SHIRLEY CHISHOLM
Brought Her Own Chair

This book belongs to

_____

"If they don't give you a seat at the table, bring a folding chair."
-Shirley Chisholm

SHIRLEY CHISHOLM
Brought Her Own Chair

By Elvie N. August

Illustrated by Amanda Marques

Shirley Anita St. Hill Chisholm was a fearless woman. She was brilliant, hardworking and determined to make the world a better place for all.

Because she was outspoken, she didn't always fit in. A lot of powerful people didn't like her guts.

But nothing and nobody could stop Shirley Chisholm.

She wanted a world where women, immigrants, the poor and ALL black and brown people could have equal treatment and opportunities.

Although some people thought Shirley was tiny in size, she found ways to be seen and heard. It was hard to miss her in a crowd.

She always wore brightly-colored clothes with patterns. Purple was her favorite.

Shirley spoke with authority and loved to debate issues that affected her community.

When she looked at you over her wide eyeglasses, you knew she meant business.

Shirley wanted to be involved in making important decisions for the country.

She wanted to be PRESIDENT of the United States of America!

Shirley's path to becoming a trailblazing leader in the U.S. wasn't easy.

Shirley was born in Brooklyn, New York. Her parents, Charles and Ruby St. Hill, worked very hard. Their jobs didn't pay them enough money to take care of Shirley and her two sisters, Odessa and Muriel.

So when Shirley was just four years old, her parents took her and her sisters on a boat to the Caribbean island of Barbados to live with their grandmother.

At first, it was difficult for Shirley to enjoy life on her grandmother's farm. She didn't fit in with the other children. Shirley missed the skyscrapers and busy streets of New York City.

But nothing and nobody could stop
Shirley Chisholm.

She tried hard and quickly came to love the open spaces and carefree life in Barbados.

Shirley helped fetch water from the well and took care of Grandma's farm animals.

Shirley enjoyed exploring the village barefoot and visiting the market with her sisters, cousins and friends.

Although she was having fun in Barbados, Shirley took her education seriously. She practiced writing even when school was out.
She never stopped dreaming of changing the world.

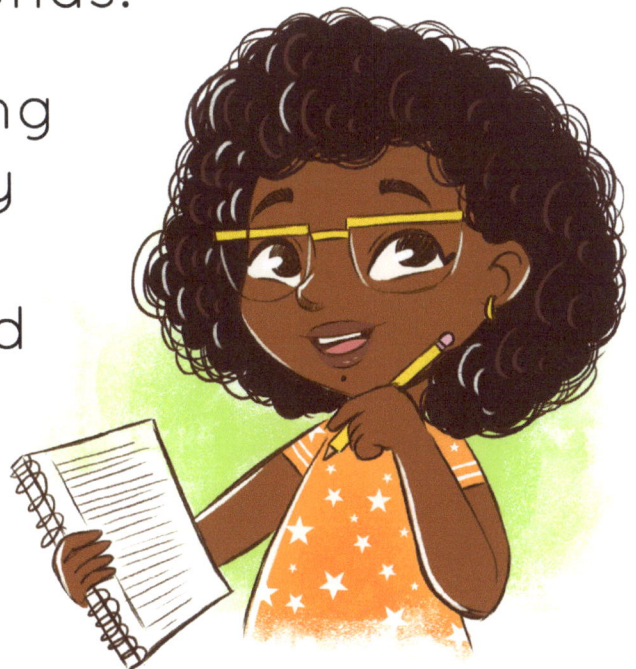

When Shirley was 10, her parents brought her and her sisters back to New York.

Shirley had a hard time fitting in again. She sounded different because she now spoke English with a Barbadian accent.

The New York streets felt crowded and the winters were too cold for her. Shirley missed the farm in Barbados.

But nothing and nobody could stop Shirley Chisholm.

She remembered what Grandma had taught her: It's okay to not always fit in.

Soon, Shirley started enjoying school in New York. She worked hard and won a scholarship to go to Brooklyn College.

Nothing and nobody can stop us!

Some clubs in the college would not allow Shirley and other African American students to join them because they were black.

So she started her own club for black female students to help them excel in their goals.

During her free time, Shirley volunteered to teach children how to draw, sew and write.

When she finished college, she became a teacher. She was also a leader in her community and the state of New York.

Shirley continued to dream of a better world for everyone. She wanted children to have healthier food and better education.

She wanted people from all backgrounds to be able to go to college and get well-paying jobs.

One day, Shirley decided to run for Congress. She wanted to fight for laws that would make the United States of America a better place for everyone.

Many people doubted her because there had never been a black woman in Congress.

But nothing and nobody could stop Shirley Chisholm.

She had to convince her community to vote for her. She knocked on doors, held rallies and talked to people on the streets.

It worked! Shirley won enough votes to become the first black female member of the United States Congress in 1969.

In Congress, some lawmakers treated Shirley poorly. They tried to exclude her and make it hard for her to fight for the things she believed in.

But nothing and nobody could stop Shirley Chisholm.

She fought back and got on committees where she could make a difference for her community.

You CAN'T

Shirley once said:

If they don't give you a seat at the table, bring a folding chair.

That was her motto.
Don't wait to be invited.

Later, Shirley decided to run for president. That was a big deal in 1972! She was the FIRST black person to seriously run for president of the United States of America.

Many people didn't want a black person and a woman to be president. Shirley knew it was going to be tough, so she picked a strong slogan for her presidential campaign: **UNBOUGHT AND UNBOSSED.**

That meant no one could make Shirley stop fighting for good.

Shirley did not win enough votes to become president, but she opened the door for girls, women and black people to run in the future.

"The next time a woman of whatever color, or a dark-skinned person of whatever sex aspires to be president, the way should be a little smoother because I helped pave it," Shirley said.

Today, a portrait of Shirley hangs on a wall in Congress. It's a reminder that nothing and nobody could stop Shirley Chisholm.

Nothing and nobody can stop YOU either!

Facts about Shirley Chisholm

- Her birthday was November 30, 1924
- She served in the New York State Assembly from 1965 to 1968
- She was a member of the U.S. Congress from 1969 to 1983
- She ran for president in 1972
- She helped create a program that still provides healthy meals for women and children
- She died on January 1, 2005 at the age of 80

About the author

Elvie N. August is a writer, educator and storyteller. She writes children's books inspired by her conversations and experiences with her two sons. In her free time, she enjoys photography and traveling.

About the illustrator

Amanda Marques is an illustrator, art director and designer. She has been passionate about animation and drawing for as long as she can remember. That has led her to an exciting career illustrating children's books.

Amanda enjoys producing art with a touch of magic that engages young readers' imaginations.

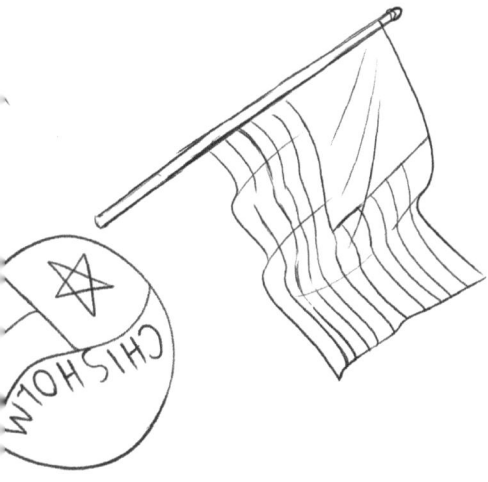

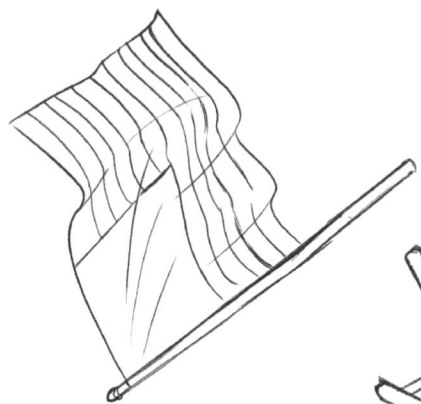

www.ingramcontent.com/pod-product-compliance
Lightning Source LLC
LaVergne TN
LVHW072133070426
835513LV00002B/84